C
from the
Heart

JAMES ALLEN TITLES

———⊙•⊙———

Out
from the
Heart

James Allen

MEDIA

Published 2019 by Gildan Media LLC
aka G&D Media
www.GandDmedia.com

Design by Meghan Day Healey of Story Horse, LLC

Library of Congress Cataloging-in-Publication Data is available upon request

ISBN: 978-1-7225-0241-6

10   9   8   7   6   5   4   3   2   1

Contents

Foreword

Confucius said, "The perfecting of one's self is the fundamental base of all progress and all moral development;" a maxim as profound and comprehensive as it is simple, practical, and uninvolved, for there is no surer way to knowledge, nor no better way to help the world than by perfecting one's self. Nor is there any nobler work or higher science than that of self-perfection. He who studies how to become faultless, who strives to be pure-hearted, who aims at the possession of a calm, wise, and seeing mind, engages in the most sublime task that man can undertake, and the results of which are perceptible in a well-ordered, blessed, and beautiful life.

—James Allen

The Heart and the Life

As the heart, so is the life. The within is ceaselessly becoming the without. Nothing remains unrevealed. That which is hidden is but for a time; it ripens and comes forth at last. Seed, tree, blossom, and fruit is the fourfold order of the universe. From the state of a man's heart proceed the conditions of his life; his thoughts blossom into deeds, and his deeds bear the fruitage of character and destiny.

Life is ever unfolding from within, and revealing itself to the light, and thoughts engendered in the heart at last reveal themselves in words, actions, and things accomplished.

As the fountain from the hidden spring, so issues man's life from the secret recesses of his heart. All that he is and does is generated there. All that he will be and do will take its rise there.

Sorrow and gladness, suffering and enjoyment, hope and fear, hatred and love, ignorance and enlightenment, are nowhere but in the heart; they are solely mental conditions.

Man is the keeper of his heart; the watcher of his mind; the solitary sentinel of his citadel of life. As such, he can be diligent or negligent. He can keep his heart more and more carefully; he can more strenuously watch and purify his mind; and he can guard himself against the thinking of unrighteous thoughts: this is the way of enlightenment and bliss. On the other hand, he can live loosely and carelessly, neglecting the supreme task of rightly ordering his life: this is the way of self-delusion and suffering.

Let a man realize that life in its totality proceeds from the mind, and lo, the way of blessedness is opened up to him! For he will then discover that he possesses the power to rule his mind, and to fashion it in accordance with his Ideal. So will be elect to strongly and steadfastly walk those pathways of thought and action which are altogether excellent; to him life will become beautiful and sacred; and, sooner or later, he will put to flight all evil, confusion and suffering; for it is impossible for a man to fall short of liberation, enlightenment, and peace, who guards with unwearying diligence the gateway of his heart.

The Nature and Power of Mind

Mind is the arbiter of life; it is the creator and shaper of conditions, and the recipient of its own results. It contains within itself both the power to create illusion and to perceive reality.

Mind is the infallible weaver of destiny; thought is the thread, good and evil deeds are the warp and woof, and the web, woven upon the loom of life, is character. Mind clothes itself in garments of its own making.

Man, as a mental being, possesses all the powers of mind, and is furnished with illimitable choice. He learns by experience, and he can accelerate or retard his experience. He is not arbitrarily bound at any point, but he has bound himself at many points, and having bound himself he can, when he chooses, liberate himself. He can become bestial or pure, ignoble or noble, foolish or wise, just as he chooses. He can, by recurring practice, form habits, and he can, by renewed effort, break them off. He can surround himself with illusions until Truth is completely lost, and he can destroy one and another of those illusions until Truth is entirely recovered. His possibilities are limitless; his freedom is complete.

It is in the nature of mind to create its own conditions, and to choose the states in which it shall dwell. It also has the power to alter any condition and to abandon any state, and this it is continually doing as it gathers knowledge of state after state by repeated choice and exhaustive experience.

Inward processes of thought make up the sum of character and life, and man can modify and alter these processes by bringing will and effort to bear upon them. The bonds of habit, impotence, and sin are self-made, and can only be destroyed by one's self; they exist nowhere but in one's mind, and although they are directly related to outward things, they have no real existence in those things. The outer is moulded and vivified by the inner, and never the inner by the outer. Temptation does not arise in the outer object, but in the lust of the mind for that object; nor do suffering and sorrow inhere in the external things and happenings of life, but in an undisciplined attitude of mind toward those things and happenings. The mind that is disciplined by Purity and fortified by Wisdom, avoids all those lusts and desires which are inseparably bound up with affliction, and so arrives at enlightenment and peace.

To condemn others as evil, and to rail against outside conditions as the source of evil, increases, and does not lessen, the world's suffering and unrest. The outer is but the shadow and effect of the inner, and when the heart is pure all outward things are pure.

All growth and life is from within outward; all decay and death is from without inward; this is a universal law. All evolution proceeds from within. All adjustment must take place within. He who ceases to strive against others, and employs his powers in the transformation, regeneration, and development of his own mind, conserves his energies and preserves himself; and as he succeeds in harmonizing his own mind, he leads others by consideration and charity into a like blessed state, for not by assuming authority and guidance over other minds is the way of enlightenment and peace discovered, but by exercising a lawful authority over one's own, and by guiding one's self in pathways of steadfast and lofty virtue.

A man's life proceeds from his heart, his mind: he has compounded that mind by his own thoughts and deeds: it is in his power to re-fashion that mind by his choice of thought: he can therefore transform his life. Let us see how this is to be done.

Formation
of Habit

Every established mental condition is an acquired habit, and it has become such by continuous repetition of thought. Despondency and cheerfulness, anger and calmness, covetousness and generosity—indeed, all states of mind—are habits built up by choice, until they have become automatic. A thought constantly repeated at last becomes a fixed habit of the mind, and from such habits proceeds the life.

It is in the nature of the mind to acquire knowledge by the repetition of its experiences. A thought which it is very difficult, at first, to hold and to dwell upon, at last becomes, by constantly being held in the mind, a natural and habitual condition. Just as a boy, when commencing to learn a trade, cannot even handle his tools aright, much less use them correctly, but after long repetition and practice plies them with perfect ease and consummate skill, so a state of mind, at first apparently impossible of realization, is, by perseverance and practice, at last acquired and built into the character as a natural and spontaneous condition.

In this power of the mind to form and re-form its habits, its conditions, is contained the basis of man's salvation, and the open door to perfect liberty by the mastery of self, for as a man has the power to form harmful habits, so he has the same power to create habits that are essentially good. And here we come to a point which needs some elucidating, and which calls for deep and earnest thought on the part of my reader.

It is commonly said to be easier to do wrong than right, to sin than to be holy; such condition has come to be regarded, almost universally, as axiomatic, and no less a teacher than the Buddha has said:—"Bad deeds, and deeds hurtful to ourselves, are easy to do; what is beneficial and good, that is very difficult to do,"—and as regards humanity generally, this is true, but it is only true as a passing experience, a fleeting factor in human evolution; it is not a fixed condition of things, is not of the nature of an eternal truth. It is easier for men to do wrong than right, because of the prevalence of ignorance, because the true nature of things, and the essence and meaning of life, are not apprehended. When a child is learning to write, it is extremely easy for it to hold the pen wrongly, and to form its letters incorrectly, but it is painfully difficult to hold the pen and to write properly; and this because of the child's ignorance of the art of writing, which can only be dispelled by persistent effort and practice, until, at last, it becomes natural and easy to hold the pen properly, and to write correctly, and difficult, as well as altogether unnecessary, to do the wrong thing. It is the same in the vital things of mind and life. To think and do rightly requires much practice and renewed effort, but the time at last comes when it becomes habitual and easy to think and do rightly, and difficult, as it is then seen to be altogether unnecessary, to do that which is wrong.

Just as an artisan becomes, by practice, accomplished in his craft, so a man can become, by practice, accomplished in goodness; it is entirely a matter of forming new habits of thought, and he to

whom right thoughts have become easy and natural, and wrong thoughts and acts difficult to do,
has attained to the highest virtue, to pure, spiritual knowledge.

It is easy and natural for men to sin, because
they have formed, by incessant repetition, harmful and unenlightened habits of thought. It is very
difficult for the thief to refrain from stealing when
opportunity occurs, because he has lived so long
in covetous and avaricious thoughts; but such
difficulty does not exist for the honest man who
has lived so long in upright and honest thoughts,
and has thereby become enlightened as to the
wrong, folly, and fruitlessness of theft, that even
the remotest idea of stealing does not enter his
mind. The sin of theft is a very extreme one, and
I have introduced it in order to the more clearly
illustrate the force and formation of habit; but
all sins and virtues are formed in the same way.
Anger and impatience are natural and easy to
thousands of people, because they are constantly
repeating the angry and impatient thought and
act, and with each repetition the habit is more
firmly established and more deeply rooted. Calmness and patience can become habitual in the
same way—by first grasping, through effort, a
calm and patient thought, and then continuously

thinking it, and living in it, until "use becomes second nature," and anger and impatience pass away for ever. It is thus that every wrong thought may be expelled from the mind; thus that every untrue act may be destroyed; thus that every sin may be overcome.

Doing and Knowing

L et a man realize that his life, in its totality, proceeds from his mind, and that that mind is a combination of habits which he can, by patient effort, modify to any extent, and over which he can thus gain complete ascendancy and control, and he has at once obtained possession of the key which shall open the door to his complete emancipation.

But emancipation from the ills of life (which are the ills of one's mind) is a matter of steady growth from within, and not a sudden acquisition from without. Hourly and daily must the mind be trained to think stainless thoughts, and to adopt right and dispassionate attitudes under those circumstances in which it is prone to fall into wrong and passion. Like the patient sculptor upon his marble, the aspirant to the Right Life must gradually work upon the crude material of his mind until he has wrought out of it the Ideal of his holiest dreams.

In working toward such supreme accomplishment, it is necessary to commence at the lowest and easiest steps, and proceed by natural and progressive stages to the higher and more difficult. This law of growth, progress, evolution, unfoldment, by gradual and ever ascending stages, is absolute in every department of life, and in every human accomplishment, and where it is ignored, total failure will result. In acquiring learning, in learning a trade, or in pursuing a business, this law is fully recognized and minutely obeyed by all; but in acquiring Virtue, in learning Truth, and in pursuing the right conduct and knowledge of life, it is unrecognized and disobeyed by nearly all; hence Virtue, Truth, and the Perfect Life remain unpractised, unacquired, and unknown.

It is a common error to suppose that the Higher Life is a matter of reading, and the adoption of theological or metaphysical hypotheses, and that Spiritual Principles can be apprehended by this method. The Higher Life is a higher living in thought, word, and deed, and the knowledge of those Spiritual Principles, which are imminent in man and in the universe can only be acquired after long discipline in the pursuit and practice of Virtue.

The lesser must be thoroughly grasped and understood before the greater can be known, and practice always precedes real knowledge. The schoolmaster never attempts to teach his pupils the abstract principles of mathematics at the commencement; he knows that by such a method teaching would be vain, and learning impossible. He first places before them a simple sum, and, having explained it, leaves them to do it. When, after repeated failures and ever-renewed effort, they have succeeded in doing it correctly, a more difficult task is set them, and then another and another; and not until the pupils have, through many years of diligent application, mastered all the lessons in arithmetic, does he attempt to unfold to them the underlying mathematical principles.

In learning a trade, say that of a mechanic, the boy is not at first taught the principles of mechanics, but a simple tool is put into his hand and he is told how rightly to use it, and is then left to do it by effort and practice. As he succeeds in plying his tools correctly, more and more difficult tasks are set him, until, after several years of successful practice, he is prepared to study and grasp the principles of mechanics.

In a properly governed household, the child is first taught to be obedient, and to conduct itself properly under all circumstances. The child is not even told why it must do this, but is commanded to do it, and only after it has so far succeeded in doing what is right and proper, is it told why it should do it. No father would attempt to teach his child the principles of ethics before exacting from it the practice of filial duty and social virtue.

Thus practice ever precedes knowledge even in the ordinary things of the world, and in spiritual things, in the living of the Higher Life, this law is rigid in its exactions. Virtue can only be known by doing, and the knowledge of Truth can only be arrived at by perfecting oneself in the practice of Virtue and to be complete in the practice and acquisition of Virtue is to complete in the knowledge of Truth.

Truth can only be arrived at by daily and hourly doing the lessons of Virtue, beginning at the simplest, and passing on to the more difficult; and as a child patiently and obediently learns its lessons at school, constantly practising, ever exerting itself until all failures and difficulties are surmounted, even so does the child of Truth apply himself to right-doing in thought and action, undaunted by failure, and made stronger by difficulties; and as he succeeds in acquiring Virtue, his mind unfolds itself in the knowledge of Truth, and it is a knowledge in which he can securely rest.

First Steps in the Higher Life

Seeing that the Path of Virtue is the Path of Knowledge, and that before the all-embracing Principles of Truth can be comprehended, perfection in the more lowly steps must be acquired, how, then, shall a disciple of Truth commence? How shall one who aspires to the righting of his mind and the purification of his heart—that heart which is the fountain and repository of all the issues of life—learn the lessons of Virtue, and thus build himself up in the strength of knowledge, destroying ignorance and the ills of life? What are the first lessons, the first steps? How are they learned? How are they practised? How are they mastered and understood?

The first lessons consist in overcoming those wrong mental conditions which are most easily eradicated, and which are the common barriers to spiritual progress, as well as in practising the simple domestic and social virtues; and the reader will be the better aided if I group and classify the first ten steps in three lessons as follows:

VICES TO BE OVERCOME AND ERADICATED.

Vices of the Body

1. Indolence.
2. Self–Indulgence.

First Lesson
Discipline of the Body

Vices of the Tongue

1. Slander.
2. Gossip and idle conversation.
3. Abusive and unkind speech.
4. Levity, or irreverent speech.
5. Captiousness, or fault-finding speech.

Second Lesson
Discipline of Speech

VIRTUES TO BE PRACTICED AND ACQUIRED.

1. Unselfish performance of duty.
2. Unswerving rectitude.
3. Unlimited forgiveness.

Third Lesson
Discipline of Inclination

The two vices of the body, and five of the tongue, are so called because they are manifested in the body and tongue, and also because, by so definitely classifying them, the mind of the reader will be the better helped; but it must be clearly understood that these vices arise primarily in the mind, and are wrong conditions of heart worked out in the body and the tongue.

The existence of such chaotic conditions is an indication that the mind is altogether unenlightened as to the real meaning and purpose of life, and their eradication is the beginning of a virtuous, steadfast, and enlightened life.

But how shall they be overcome and eradicated? By first, and at once, checking and controlling their outward manifestations, by suppressing the wrong act; this will stimulate the mind to watchfulness and reflection until, by repeated practice, it will at last come to perceive and understand the dark and wrong conditions of mind, out of which such acts spring, and will abandon them entirely.

It will be seen that the first step in the discipline of the mind is the overcoming of indolence. This is the easiest step, and until it is perfectly accomplished, the other steps cannot he taken. The clinging to indolence constitues a complete barrier to the Path of Truth. Indolence consists in giving the body more ease and sleep than it requires, in procrastinating, and in shirking and neglecting those things which should receive immediate attention. This condition of laziness must be overcome by rousing up the body at any early hour, giving it just the amount of sleep it requires for complete recuperation, and by doing promptly and vigorously, every task and duty, no matter how small, as it comes along. On no account should food or drink be taken in bed, and to lie in bed after one has wakened, indulging in ease and reverie, is a habit fatal to promptness and resolution of character, and purity of mind. Nor should one attempt to do his thinking at such a time. Strong, pure, and true thinking is impossible under such circumstances. A man should go to bed to sleep, not to think. He should get up to think and work, not to sleep.

The next step is the overcoming of self-indulgence, or gluttony. The glutton is he who eats for animal gratification only, without considering the true end and object in eating, who eats more than his body requires, and is greedy after sweet things and rich dishes. Such undisciplined desire can only be overcome by reducing the quantity of food eaten, and the number of meals per day, and by resorting to a simple and uninvolved dietary. Regular hours should be set apart for meals, and eating at other times should be rigidly avoided. Suppers should be abolished, as they are altogether unnecessary, and conduce to heavy sleep and cloudiness of mind. The pursuit of such a method of discipline will rapidly bring the hitherto ungoverned appetite under control, and as the sensual sin of self-indulgence is taken out of the mind, the right selection of food will be instinctively and infallibly adapted to the purified mental condition.

It should be well borne in mind that change of heart is the needful thing, and that any change of diet which does not subserve this end is futile. Whilst one eats for enjoyment he is gluttonous. The heart must be purified of sensual craving and gustatory lust.

When the body is well controlled and firmly guided; when that which is to be done is done vigorously; when no task or duty is delayed; when early rising has become a delight; when frugality, temperance, and abstinence are firmly established; when one is contented with the food which is put before him, no matter how scanty and plain, and the craving for gustatory pleasure is at an end—then are the first two steps in the Higher Life accomplished; then is the first great lesson in Truth learned. Thus is established in the heart the foundation of a poised, self-governed, virtuous life.

The next lesson is the lesson of Virtuous Speech, in which are five orderly steps. The first step is the overcoming of slander. Slander consists in inventing or repeating evil reports about others, in exposing and magnifying the faults of others, or of absent friends, and in introducing unworthy insinuations. The elements of thoughtlessness, cruelty, insincerity, and untruthfulness enter into every slanderous act. He who aims at the living of the right life will commence to check the cruel word of slander before it has gone forth from his lips, and will then check and eliminate the insincere thought which gave rise to it. He will watch himself that he does not vilify any, and will refrain from disparaging and condemning the absent friend, whose face he has so recently kissed, or shaken his hand, or smiled into his face. He will not say of another that which he dare not say to him. Thus, coming at last to think sacredly of the character and reputation of others, he will destroy those wrong conditions of mind which give rise to slander.

The next step is the overcoming of gossip and idle conversation. Idle speech consists in talking about the private affairs of others, in talking merely to pass away the time, and in engaging in aimless and irrelevant conversation. Such an ungoverned condition of speech is the outcome of an ill-regulated mind. The man of virtue will bridle his tongue, and thus learn how rightly to govern the mind. He will not let his tongue run idly and foolishly, but will make his speech strong and pure and will either talk with a purpose or remain silent.

Abusive and unkind speech is the next vice to be overcome. The man who abuses and accuses others has himself wandered far from the Right Way. To hurl hard words and names at others is to sink deeply into folly. When a man is inclined to abuse and condemn others, let him restrain his tongue and look in upon himself. The virtuous man refrains from abuse and quarrelling, and employs only words that are useful, necessary, pure, and true.

The next step is the overcoming of levity, or irreverent speech. Light and frivolous talking; the repeating of coarse jokes; the telling of vulgar stories, having no other purpose than to raise an empty laugh; offensive familiarity, and the employment of contemptuous and irreverent terms when speaking to or of others, and particularly of one's elders and those who rank as one's teachers, guardians, or superiors,—all this will be put away by the lover of Virtue and Truth.

Upon the altar of irreverence absent friends and companions are immolated for the passing excitement of a momentary laugh, and all the sanctity of life is sacrificed to the zest for ridicule. When respect toward others and the giving of reverence where reverence is due are abandoned, Virtue is abandoned. When modesty, gravity, and dignity are eliminated from speech and behavior, Truth is lost, yea, even its entrance gate is hidden away and forgotten. Irreverence is degrading even in the young, but when it accompanies grey hairs, and appears in the demeanor of the preacher,—this is indeed a piteous spectacle; and when this can be imitated and followed after, then are the blind leading the blind, then have elders and preacher and people lost their way.

The virtuous man will be of grave and reverent speech; he will think and speak of the absent as he thinks and speaks of the dead—tenderly and sacredly; he will put away thoughtlessness, and watch that he does not sacrifice his dignity to gratify a passing impulse to lightness and frivolity. His mirth will be pure and innocent, and his voice will become subdued and musical, and his soul be filled with grace and sweetness as he succeeds in conducting himself as becomes a man of Truth.

The last step in the second lesson is the overcoming of captiousness, or fault-finding speech. This vice of the tongue consists in magnifying and harping on small or apparent faults, in foolish quibbling and hair-splitting, and in pursuing vain arguments based upon groundless suppositions, beliefs, and opinions. Life is short and real, and sin and sorrow and pain are not remedied by carping and contention. The man who is ever on the watch to catch at the words of others in order to contradict and controvert them, has yet to reach the higher way of holiness, the truer life of self-surrender. The man who is ever on the watch to check his own words in order to soften and purify them will find the higher way and the truer life; he will conserve his energies, maintain his composure of mind, and preserve within himself the spirit of Truth.

When the tongue is well controlled and wisely subdued; when selfish impulses and unworthy thoughts no longer rush to the tongue demanding utterance; when the speech has become harmless, pure, gentle, gracious, and purposeful, and no word is uttered but in sincerity and truth,—then are the five steps in virtuous speech accomplished, then is the second great lesson in Truth learned and mastered.

And now some will ask, "But why all this discipline of the body and restraint of the tongue? Surely the Higher Life can be realized and known

without such strenuous labor, such incessant effort
and watchfulness?" No, it cannot. In the spiritual
as the material, nothing is done without labor,
and the higher cannot be known until the lower
is fufilled. Can a man make a table before he has
learned how to handle a tool and drive a nail? And
can a man fashion his mind in accordance with
Truth before he has overcome the slavery of his
body? As the intricate subtleties of language cannot be apprehended and wielded before the alpha-
bet and the simplest words are mastered, neither
can the deep subtleties of the mind be understood
and purified before the A B C of right conduct is
perfectly acquired. As for the labor involved—does
not the youth joyfully and patiently submit himself to a seven-years' apprenticeship in order to
master a craft? And does he not day by day carefully and faithfully carry out every detail of his
master's instructions, looking forward to the time
when, perfected through obedience and practice,
he shall be himself a master? Where is the man
who sincerely aims at excellence in music, paint-
ing, literature, in any trade, business, or profes-
sion who is not willing to give his whole life to the
acquirement of his particular perfection? Shall
labor, then, be considered where the very highest
excellence is concerned—the excellence of Truth?
He who says, "The Path which you point out is too

difficult; I must have Truth without labor, salvation without effort," that man will not find his way out of the confusions and sufferings of self-hood; he will not find the calm and well-fortified mind and the wisely ordered life. His love is for ease and enjoyment, and not for Truth. He who, deep in his heart, adores Truth, and aspires to know it, will consider no labor too great to be undertaken, but will adopt it joyfully and pursue it patiently, and by perseverance in practice he will come to the knowledge of Truth.

The necessity for this preliminary discipline of the body and tongue will be the more clearly perceived when it is fully understood that all these wrong outward conditions are merely the expressions of wrong conditions of heart. An indolent body means an indolent mind; an ill-regulated tongue reveals an ill-regulated mind, and the process of remedying the manifested condition is really a method of rectifying the inward state. Moreover, the overcoming of these conditions is only a small part of what is really involved in the process. The ceasing from evil leads to, and is inseparably connected with, the practice of good. While a man is overcoming indolence and self-indulgence, he is really cultivating and developing the virtues of abstinence, temperance, punctuality, and self-denial, and is acquiring that strength, energy, and resolution which are indispensable to the successful accomplishment of the higher tasks. While he is overcoming the vices of speech, he is developing the virtues of truthfulness, sincerity, reverence, kindliness, and self-control, and is gaining that mental steadiness and fixedness of purpose, without which the remoter subtleties of the mind cannot be regulated, and the higher stages of conduct and enlightenment cannot be reached. Also, as he has to do right, his knowledge deepens, and his insight is intensified, and as the child's heart is glad when his school task is mastered, so with each victory achieved, the man of virtue experiences a bliss which the seeker after pleasure and excitement can never know.

And now we come to the third lesson in the Higher Life, which consists in practising and mastering, in one's daily life, three great fundamental. Virtues—(1) Unselfish Performance of Duty; (2) Unswerving Rectitude; and (3) Unlimited Forgiveness. Having prepared the mind by overcoming the more surface and chaotic conditions mentioned in the two first lessons, the striver after Virtue and Truth is now ready to enter upon greater and more difficult tasks, and to control and purify the deeper motives of the heart. Without the right performance of duty, the higher virtues cannot be known, and Truth cannot be apprehended. Duty is generally regarded as an irksome labor, a compulsory something which must be toiled through, or be in some way circumvented. This way of regarding Duty proceeds from a selfish condition of mind, and a wrong understanding of life. All duty should be regarded as sacred, and its faithful and unselfish performance one of the leading rules of conduct. All personal and selfish considerations should be extracted and cast away from the doing of one's duty, and when this is done, Duty ceases to be irksome, and becomes joyful. Duty is only irksome to him who craves some selfish enjoyment or benefit for himself. Let the man who is chafing under the irksomeness of his duty look to himself, and he will find that his wearisomeness proceeds, not from the duty itself, but from his selfish desire to escape it. He who neglects duty, be it great or small, or of a public or private nature, neglects Virtue; he who in his heart rebels against Duty, rebels against Virtue. When Duty has become a thing of love, and when every particular duty is done accurately, faithfully, and dispassionately, there is much subtle selfishness removed from the heart, and a great step is taken toward the heights of Truth. The virtuous man concentrates his mind on the perfect doing of his own duty, and does not interfere with the duty of another.

The second step in the third lesson is the practice of Unswerving Rectitude. This Virtue must be firmly established in the mind, and so enter into every detail of man's life. All dishonesty, deception, trickery, and misrepresentation must be for ever put away, and the heart be purged of every vestige of insincerity and subterfuge. The least swerving from the path of rectitude is a deviation from Virtue. There must be no extravagance and exaggeration of speech, but the simple truth should be stated. Engaging in deception, no matter how apparently insignificant, for vain-glory, or with the hope of personal advantage, is a state of delusion which one should make efforts to dispel. It is demanded of the man of Virtue that he shall not only practice the most rigid honesty in thought, word, and deed, but that he shall be exact in his statements, omitting and adding nothing to the actual truth. In thus shaping his mind to the principle of Rectitude, he will gradually come to deal with people and things in a just and impartial spirit, considering equity before himself, and viewing all things with freedom from personal bias, passion, and prejudice. When the Virtue of Rectitude is fully practised, acquired, and comprehended, so that all temptation to untruthfulness and insincerity has ceased, then is the heart made purer and nobler, then is character strengthened, and knowledge enlarged, and life takes on a new meaning and a new power. Thus is the second step accomplished.

The third step is the practice of Unlimited Forgiveness. This consists in overcoming the sense of injury which springs from vanity, selfishness, and pride; and in exercising disinterested charity and large-heartedness toward all. Spite, retaliation, and revenge are so utterly ignoble, and so small and foolish, as to be altogether unworthy of being noticed or harbored. No one who fosters such conditions in his heart can lift himself above folly and suffering, and guide his life aright. Only by casting them away, and ceasing to be moved by them, can a man's eyes be opened to the true way in life; only by developing a forgiving and charitable spirit can he hope to approach and perceive the strength and beauty of a well-ordered life. In the heart of the strongly virtuous man no feeling of personal injury can arise; he has put away all retaliation, and has no enemies; and if men should constitute themselves his enemies, he will regard them kindly, understanding their ignorance, and making full allowance for it. When this state of heart is arrived at, then is the third step in the discipline of one's self-seeking inclinations accomplished; then is the third great lesson in Virtue and Knowledge learned and mastered.

Having thus laid down the first ten steps and three lessons in right-doing and right-knowing, I leave those of my readers who are prepared for them to learn and master them in their everyday life. There is, of course, a still higher discipline of the body, a more far-reaching discipline of the tongue, and greater and more all-embracing virtues to acquire and understand before the highest state of bliss and knowledge can be apprehended, but it is not my purpose to deal with them here. I have expounded only the first and easiest lessons on the Higher Path, and by the time these are thoroughly mastered, the reader will have become so purified, strengthened, and enlightened, that he will not be left in the dark as to his future progress. Those of my readers who have completed these three lessons will already have perceived, beyond and above, the high altitudes of Truth, and the narrow and precipitous track which leads to them, and will choose whether they shall proceed.

The straight Path which I have laid down can be pursued by all with greater profit to themselves and to the world, and even those who do not aspire to the attainment of Truth, will develop greater intellectual and moral strength, finer judgment, and deeper peace of mind by perfecting themselves in this Path. Nor will their material prosperity suffer by this change of heart; nay, it will be rendered truer, purer, and more enduring, for if there is one who is capable of succeeding and fitted to achieve, it is the man who has abandoned the petty dissipations and everyday vices of his kind, who is strong to rule his body and his mind, and who pursues with fixed resolve the path of unswerving integrity and sterling virtue.

Mental
Conditions
and Their Effects

Without going into the details of the greater steps and lessons in the right life (a task outside the scope of this small work) a few hints and statements concerning those mental conditions from which life in its totality springs, will prove helpful to those who are ready and willing to penetrate further into that inner realm of heart and mind where Love and Wisdom and Peace await the strenuous comer.

All sin is ignorance. It is a condition of darkness and undevelopment. The wrong-thinker and wrong-doer is in the same position in the school of

life as is the ignorant pupil in the school of learning. He has yet to learn how to think and act correctly, that is, in accordance with Law. The pupil
in learning is not happy so long as he does his lessons wrongly, and unhappiness cannot be escaped
while sin remains unconquered.

Life is a series of lessons. Some are diligent in
learning them, and they become pure, wise, and
altogether happy. Others are negligent, and do not
apply themselves, and they remain impure, foolish, and unhappy.

Every form of unhappiness springs from a
wrong condition of mind. Happiness inheres in
right conditions of mind. Happiness is mental har-
mony; unhappiness is mental inharmony. While a
man lives in wrong conditions of mind, he will live
a wrong life, and will suffer continually. Suffering
is rooted in error. Bliss inheres in enlightenment.
There is salvation for man only in the destruction
of his own ignorance, error, and self-delusion.
Where there are wrong conditions of mind there is
bondage and unrest; where there are right conditions of mind there is freedom and peace.

Here are some of the leading wrong mental conditions and their disastrous effects upon the life:

Wrong Mental Conditions	Their Effects
Hatred	Injury, violence, disaster, and suffering.
Lust	Confusion of intellect, remorse, shame, and wretchedness.
Covetousness	Fear, unrest, unhappiness, and loss.
Pride	Disappointment, chagrin, lack of self-knowledge.
Vanity	Distress, and mortification of spirit.
Condemnation	Persecution, hatred from others.
Ill-will	Failures and troubles.
Self-indulgence	Misery, loss of judgment, grossness, disease, and neglect.
Anger	Loss of power and influence.
Desire, or Self-slavery	Grief, folly, sorrow, uncertainty, and loneliness.

The above wrong conditions of mind are merely negations; they are states of darkness and deprivation and not of positive power. Evil is not a power; it is ignorance and misuse of good. The hater is he who has failed to do the lesson of Love correctly, and he suffers in consequence. When he succeeds in doing it rightly, the hatred will have disappeared, and he will see and understand the darkness and impotence of hatred. It is so with every wrong condition.

The following are some of the more important right mental conditions and their beneficent effects upon the life:

Right Mental Conditions	Their Effects
Love	Gentle conditions, bliss, and blessedness.
Purity	Intellectual clearness, joy, invincible confidence.
Selflessness	Courage, satisfaction, happiness, and plenty.
Humility	Calmness, restfulness, knowledge of Truth.
Meekness	Equipoise, contentment under all circumstances.
Compassion	Protection, love and reverence from others.
Goodwill	Gladness and success.
Self-control	Peace of mind, true judgment, refinement, health, and honor.
Patience	Mental power, far-reaching influence.
Self-conquest	Enlightenment, wisdom, insight, and profound peace.

These conditions of mind are states of positive power, of light, of joyful possession, and of knowledge. The good man knows. He has learned to do his lessons correctly, and thereby understands the exact proportions which make up the sum of life. He is enlightened, and knows good and evil. He is supremely happy, doing only that which is divinely right.

The man who is involved in the wrong conditions of mind, does not know. He is ignorant of good and evil, of himself, of the inward causes which make his life. He is unhappy, and believes other people are entirely the cause of his unhappiness. He works blindly, and lives in darkness, seeing no central purpose in existence, and no orderly and lawful sequence in the course of things.

He who aspires to the attainment of the Higher Life in its completion—who would perceive with unveiled vision the true order of things and the meaning of life—let him abandon all the wrong conditions of heart, and persevere unceasingly in the practice of the good. If he suffers, or doubts, or is unhappy, let him search within until he finds the cause, and having found it, let him cast it away. Let him so guard and purify his heart that every day less of evil and more of good shall issue therefrom; so will he daily become stronger, nobler, wiser; so will his blessedness increase, and the Light of Truth, growing ever brighter and brighter within him, will dispel all gloom, and illuminate his Pathway.

Exhortation

Disciples of Truth, lovers of Virtue, seekers of Wisdom; ye, also, who are sorrow stricken, knowing the emptiness of the self-life, and who aspire to the life that is supremely beautiful, and serenely glad,—take now yourselves in hand, enter the Door of Discipline, and know the Better Life.

Put away self-delusion; behold yourself as you are, and see the Path of Virtue as it is. There is no lazy way to Truth. He who would stand upon the mountain's summit must strenuously climb, and must rest only to gather strength. But if the climbing is less glorious than the cloudless summit, it is still glorious. Discipline in itself is beautiful, and the end of discipline is sweet.

Rise early and meditate. Begin each day with a conquered body, and a mind fortified against error and weakness. Temptation will never be overcome by unprepared fighting. The mind must be armed and arrayed in the silent hour. It must be trained to perceive, to know, to understand. Sin and temptation disappear when right understanding is developed.

Right understanding is reached through unabated discipline. Truth cannot be reached but through discipline. Patience will increase by effort and practice, and patience will make discipline beautiful.

Discipline is irksome to the impatient man and the self-lover, so he avoids it, and continues to live loosely and confusedly.

Discipline is not irksome to the Truth-lover, and he will find the Infinite patience which can wait and work and overcome. As the joy of the gardener who sees his flowers develop day by day, so is the joy of the man of discipline who sees the divine flowers of Purity, Wisdom, Compassion, and Love, grow up in his heart.

The loose-liver cannot escape sorrow and pain. The undisciplined mind falls, weak and helpless, before the fierce onslaught of passion.

Array well your mind, then, lover of Truth. Be watchful, thoughtful, resolute. Your salvation is at hand; your readiness and effort are all that are needed. If you should fail ten times, do not be disheartened; if you should fail a hundred times, rise up and pursue your way; if you should fail a thousand times, do not despair. When the right Path is entered, success is sure if the Path is not utterly abandoned.

First strife, and then victory. First labor, and then rest. First weakness, and then strength. In the beginning the lower life, and the glare and confusion of battle, and at the end the Life Beautiful, the Silence, and the Peace.

James Allen: A Memoir

By Lily L. Allen

from *The Epoch* (February–March 1912)

> *Unto pure devotion*
> *Devote thyself: with perfect meditation*
> *Comes perfect act, and the right-hearted rise—*
> *More certainly because they seek no gain—*
> *Forth from the bands of body, step by step.*
> *To highest seats of bliss.*

James Allen was born in Leicester, England, on November 28th, 1864. His father, at one time a very prosperous manufacturer, was especially fond of "Jim," and before great financial failures overtook him, he would often look at the delicate, refined boy, poring over his books, and would say, "My boy, I'll make a scholar of you."

The Father was a high type of man intellectually, and a great reader, so could appreciate the evident thirst for education and knowledge which he observed in his quiet studious boy.

As a young child he was very delicate and nervous, often suffering untold agony during his school days through the misunderstanding harshness of some of his school teachers, and others with whom he was forced to associate, though he retained always the tenderest memories of others—one or two of his teachers in particular, who no doubt are still living.

He loved to get alone with his books, and many a time he has drawn a vivid picture for me, of the hours he spent with his precious books in his favourite corner by the home fire; his father, whom he dearly loved, in his arm chair opposite also deeply engrossed in his favourite authors. On such evenings he would question his father on some of the profound thoughts that surged through his soul—thoughts he could scarcely form into words—and the father, unable to answer, would gaze at him long over his spectacles, and at last say: "My boy, my boy, you have lived before"—and when the boy eagerly but reverently would suggest an answer to his own question, the father would grow silent and thoughtful, as though he *sensed* the future man and his mission, as he looked at the boy and listened to his words—and many a time he was heard to remark, "Such knowledge comes not in one short life."

There were times when the boy startled those about him into a deep concern for his health, and they would beg him not to *think so much*, and in after years he often smiled when he recalled how his father would say—"Jim, we will have you in the Churchyard soon, if you think so much."

Not that he was by any means unlike other boys where games were concerned. He could play leap-frog and marbles with the best of them, and those who knew him as a man—those who were privileged to meet him at "Bryngoleu"—will remember how he could enter into a game with all his heart. Badminton he delighted in during the summer evenings, or whenever he felt he could.

About three years after our marriage, when our little Nora was about eighteen months old, and he about thirty-three, I realized a great change coming over him, and knew that he was renouncing everything that most men hold dear that he might find Truth, and lead the weary sin-stricken world to Peace. He at that time commenced the practice of rising early in the morning, at times long before daylight, that he might go out on the hills—like One of old—to commune with God, and meditate on Divine things. I do not claim to have understood him fully in those days. The light in which he lived and moved was far too white for my earth-bound eyes to see, and a *sense of it only* was beginning to dawn upon me. But I knew I dare not stay him or hold him back, though at times my woman's heart cried out to do so, waiting him all my own, and not then understanding his divine mission.

Then came his first book, "From Poverty to Power." This book is considered by many his best book. It has passed into many editions, and tens of thousands have been sold all over the world, both authorized and pirated editions, for perhaps no author's works have been more pirated than those of James Allen.

As a private secretary he worked from 9 a.m. to 6 p.m., and used every moment out of office writing his books. Soon after the publication of "From Poverty to Power" came "All These Things Added," and then "As a Man Thinketh," a book perhaps better known and more widely read than any other from his pen.

About this time, too, the "Light of Reason" was founded and he gave up all his time to the work of editing the Magazine, at the same time carrying on a voluminous correspondence with searchers after Truth all over the world. And ever as the years went by he kept straight on, and never once looked back or swerved from the path of holiness. Oh, it was a blessed thing indeed to be the chosen one to walk by the side of his earthly body, and to watch the glory dawning upon him!

He took a keen interest in many scientific subjects, and always eagerly read the latest discovery in astronomy, and he delighted in geology and botany. Among his favourite books I find Shakespeare, Milton, Emerson, Browning, The Bhagavad-Gita, the Tao-Tea-King of Lao-Tze, the Light of Asia, the Gospel of Buddha, Walt Whitman, Dr. Bucke's Cosmic Consciousness, and the Holy Bible.

He might have written on a wide range of subjects had he chosen to do so, and was often asked for articles on many questions outside his particular work, but he refused to comply, consecrating his whole thought and effort to preach the Gospel of Peace.

When physical suffering overtook him he never once complained, but grandly and patiently bore his pain, hiding it from those around him, and only we who knew and loved him so well, and his kind, tender Doctor, knew how greatly he suffered. And yet he stayed not; still he rose before the dawn to meditate, and commune with God; still he sat at his desk and wrote those words of Light and Life which will ring down through the ages, calling men and women from their sins and sorrows to peace and rest.

Always strong in his complete manhood, though small of stature physically, and as gentle as he was strong, no one ever heard an angry word from those kind lips. Those who served him adored him; those who had business dealings with him trusted and honoured him. Ah! how much my heart prompts me to write of his self-sacrificing life, his tender words, his gentle deeds, his knowledge and his wisdom. But why? Surely there is no need, for do not his books speak in words written by his own hand, and will they not speak to generations yet to come?

About Christmas time I saw the change coming, and understood it not—blind! blind! blind! I could not think it possible that *he* should be taken and *I* left.

But we three—as if we knew—clung closer to each other, and loved one another with a greater love—if that were possible—than ever before. Look at his portrait given with the January "Epoch," and reproduced again in this, and you will see that even then our Beloved, our Teacher and Guide, was letting go his hold on the physical. He was leaving us then, and we didn't know it. Often I had urged him to stop work awhile and rest, but he always gave me the same answer, "My darling, when I stop I must go, don't try to stay my hand."

And so he worked on, until that day, Friday, January 12, 1912, when, about one o'clock he sat down in his chair, and looking at me with a great compassion and yearning in those blessed eyes, he cried out, as he stretched out his arms to me, *"Oh, I have finished, I have finished, I can go no further, I have done."*

Need I say that everything that human aid and human skill could do was done to keep him still with us. Of those last few days I dare scarcely write. How could my pen describe them? And when we knew the end was near, with his dear hands upon my head in blessing, he gave his work and his beloved people into my hands, charging me to bless and help them, until I received the call to give up my stewardship!

"I will help you," he said, "and if I can I shall come to you and be with you often."

Words, blessed words of love and comfort, *for my heart alone* often came from his lips, and a sweet smile ever came over the pale calm face when our little Nora came to kiss him and speak loving words to him, while always the gentle voice breathed the tender words to her—*"My little darling!"*

So calmly, peacefully, quietly, he passed from us at the dawn on Wednesday, January 24, 1912. "Passed from us," did I say? Nay, only the outer garment has passed from our mortal vision. He lives! and when the great grief that tears our hearts at the separation is calmed and stilled, I think that we shall know that he is still with us. We shall again rejoice in his companionship and presence.

When his voice was growing faint and low, I heard him whispering, and leaning down to catch the words I heard—"At last, at last—at home—my wanderings are over"—and then, I heard no more, for my heart was breaking within me, and I felt, for *him* indeed it was "*Home at last!*" but for me—And then, as though he knew my thoughts, he turned and again holding out his hands to me, he said: "I have only one thing more to say to you, my beloved, and that is I love you, and I will be waiting for you; good-bye."

I write this memoir for those who love him, for those who will read it with tender loving hearts, and tearful eyes; for those who will not look critically at the way in which I have tried to tell out of my lonely heart this short story of his life and passing away—for *his* pupils, and, therefore, my friends.

We clothed the mortal remains in *pure white linen*, symbol of his fair, pure life, and so, clasping the photo of the one he loved best upon his bosom—they committed all that remained to the funeral pyre.

About the Author

James Allen was one of the pioneering figures of the self-help movement and modern inspirational thought. A philosophical writer and poet, he is best known for his book *As a Man Thinketh*. Writing about complex subjects such as faith, destiny, love, patience, and religion, he had the unique ability to explain them in a way that is simple and easy to comprehend. He often wrote about cause and effect, as well as overcoming sadness, sorrow and grief.

Allen was born in 1864 in Leicester, England into a working-class family. His father travelled alone to America to find work, but was murdered within days of arriving. With the family now facing economic disaster, Allen, at age 15, was forced to leave school and find work to support them.

During stints as a private secretary and stationer, he found that he could showcase his spiritual and social interests in journalism by writing for the magazine *The Herald of the Golden Age.*

In 1901, when he was 37, Allen published his first book, *From Poverty to Power.* In 1902 he began to publish his own spiritual magazine, *The Light of Reason* (which would be retitled *The Epoch* after his death). Each issue contained announcements, an editorial written by Allen on a different subject each month, and many articles, poems, and quotes written by popular authors of the day and even local, unheard of authors.

His third and most famous book *As a Man Thinketh* was published in 1903. The book's minor popularity enabled him to quit his secretarial work and pursue his writing and editing career full time. He wrote 19 books in all, publishing at least one per year while continuing to publish his magazine, until his death. Allen wrote when he had a message—one that he had lived out in his own life and knew that it was good.

In 1905, Allen organized his magazine subscribers into groups (called "The Brotherhood") that would meet regularly and reported on their meetings each month in the magazine. Allen and his wife, Lily Louisa Oram, whom he had married in 1895, would often travel to these group meetings to give speeches and read articles. Some of Allen's favorite writings, and those he quoted often, include the works of Shakespeare, Milton, Emerson, the Bible, Buddha, Whitman, Trine, and Lao-Tze.

Allen died in 1912 at the age of 47. Following his death, Lily, with the help of their daughter, Nora took over the editing of *The Light of Reason*, now under the name *The Epoch*. Lily continued to publish the magazine until her failing eyesight prevented her from doing so. Lily's life was devoted to spreading the works of her husband until her death at age 84.